Doll Tees

Sparkling shirts to make your doll shine!

★ American Girl®

Questions or comments? Call 1-800-845-0005,
visit our Web site at **americangirl.com**,
or write to Customer Service, American Girl, 8400 Fairway Place, Middleton, WI 53562-0497.

Printed in China

09 10 11 12 13 14 LEO 13 12 11 10 9 8

All American Girl marks are trademarks of American Girl, LLC.

Editorial Development: Trula Magruder

Art Direction and Design: Camela Decaire

Production: Mindy Rappe, Kendra Schluter, Jeannette Bailey, Judith Lary

Illustrations: Casey Lukatz

Photography: Radlund Photography

Stylists: Mandy Crary, Pam Retelle

Dear Doll Lover,

Explore your doll's passion for fashion with these
easy-to-make tees.

Planning a party? Crazy about critters? Taking a summer
trip? These sweet styles will put a big smile on your doll's
face. Just flip through the designs, find a trio of terrific
choices, and have fun!

Your Friends at American Girl

Getting Started

Fashion designers know their stuff! Here's what *you* need to know.

Rub-Off Warning!

One of the most important things to learn about creating doll clothes is that some dyes can rub off onto a doll's fabric and vinyl. Colors from ribbons, materials, and felts may bleed onto the doll and cause *permanent* stains.

The craft materials included and shown in this kit will not stain your doll. If we didn't use a sparkly red felt, it's because the red felt stained during our testing.

If you use store-bought craft supplies or shirts on your doll, be sure to check your doll often to make sure the colors aren't transferring to her body or vinyl. And never get your doll wet! Water greatly increases the risk of dye rub-off.

Don't Wash!

Never wash your designed tees—they will not hold up to machine or hand washing. If you get a stain on an area not near the design, you can ask a parent to help you spot wash it. Avoid sticky fingers, rough play, dirt, and water, and your tee designs will last longer.

T-Shirt Board

Your kit includes a T-shirt board to keep the front of your doll tee flat while you're working, and to prevent glue from bleeding through to the shirt back. Let your design dry a short time with the board in place. Then remove the board and let the tee dry completely flat.

Tweezers

Tweezers can help you to position gems, sequins, and other small crafting supplies.

Tacky Craft Glue Works Best

Since these T-shirts shouldn't be washed, you won't need to use fabric glue. Tacky craft glues are easier to control than runny fabric glues.

Use a toothpick to apply glue to gems, sequins, thin ribbon, and other small objects.

Never decorate a tee while your doll is wearing it! All the glue must be completely dry before you slip the shirt on your doll—otherwise your doll may end up wearing the shirt permanently. Use your T-shirt board, and work in an area approved by a parent.

Plan your designs carefully. If you place a design in the wrong spot and then try to move it, you'll end up with messy glue stains.

Tee Template

Fashion designers draw their creations before they make them. You can, too! Plan your own T-shirt design here before you make one.

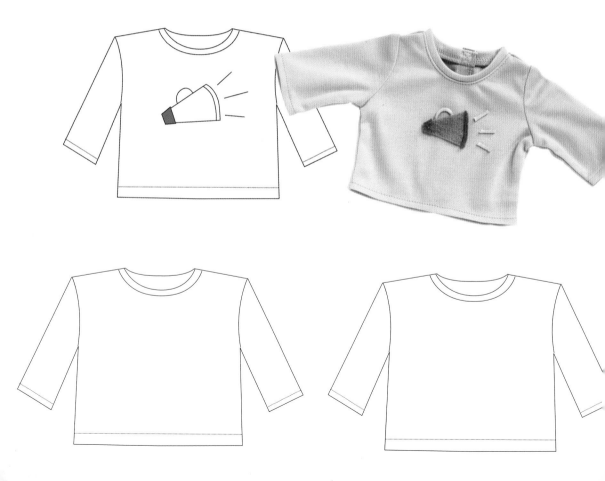

In the Fields

Perfect patterns for parks, picnics, and picking flowers

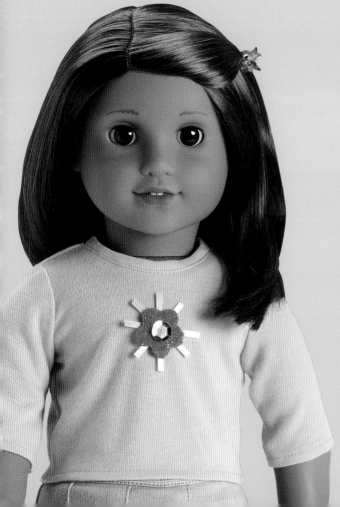

Blue Bud

Slip a tee onto the T-shirt board.
1. Crisscross light blue ribbon strips, and glue them on as shown. 2. Add a sparkly blue felt flower (pattern on page 30). 3. Glue on a round silver sequin. Let dry.

Peewee Posy

Slip a tee onto the board. Glue purple gems around a blue gem. Let dry.

Inchworm

Slip a tee onto the board. 1. Glue on a small piece of green chenille rickrack for a body. 2. Add a green button head. 3. Glue on green satin cord for antennae. 4. Glue tiny gems to the antennae. Let dry.

Puffballs

Slip a tee onto the board. 1. Glue on sparkly pink mini pom-poms as shown. 2. Add a green satin cord for a stem. Let dry.

Tee Party

Bright blouses for birthdays, babysitting, and bake sales

Fluffy Cupcake

Slip a tee onto the board. **1.** For a cupcake, glue on a tan felt strip for cake, a sparkly pink felt bottom for a cup (trim the top with pinking shears), and white felt for frosting. **2.** For a candle, glue on thin pink ribbon and a gold gem. Let dry.

Bitty Balloons

Slip a tee onto the board. **1.** Glue on thin blue ribbon strips for strings and then large purple and blue teardrop gems for balloons. **2.** Finish with a pink ribbon bow. Let dry.

Glittery Gift

Slip a tee onto the board. **1.** For a gift, cut a square from sparkly pink felt. Then crisscross blue ribbon strips, gluing the ends to the back of the gift. Glue the gift to the tee. **2.** Tie a ribbon bow, and glue it to the gift. Let dry.

All Heart

Sweet styles for scrapbooking, show-and-tell, and Saint Valentine's

Heart Art

Slip a tee onto the board. 1. Cut out a sparkly purple felt heart (pattern on page 30). **2.** Glue colored mini pom-poms around the heart edge. **3.** Glue purple gems to the heart. Let dry.

I ♥ Ice Cream

Slip a tee onto the board. 1. Make an "I" using pink ribbon strips. **2.** Cut out "vanilla" and "strawberry" ice cream shapes from sparkly pink and white felt. **3.** Cut out a cone from tan felt. **4.** Glue on all the pieces, including the heart sequin, as shown. Let dry.

Candy Heart

Slip a tee onto the board. 1. Cut out a sparkly pink felt heart. **2.** Glue a cute message to the heart using letter beads. Let dry.

Hippity-Hop

Fitting features for fishing, field trips, and fun in the sun

Fat Frog

Slip a tee onto the board. **1.** Cut out frog legs from green felt (pattern on page 30), and glue them on the tee. **2.** Add a large, round green gem for a body. **3.** Glue on small green beads for eyes. Let dry.

Bunny Tail

Slip a tee onto the board. 1. Cut out a
bunny from sparkly gray felt (pattern on
page 30). 2. Glue the bunny to the tee.
3. Add a white mini pom-pom tail. Let dry.

Winged Things

Creature collections for cookouts, catching bugs, and camping

My Butterfly

Slip a tee onto the board. **1.** Glue on a row of yellow gems as shown. **2.** Make wings with small orange buttons on top and large orange buttons on the bottom. **3.** Use black satin cord for antennae. Let dry.

Ladybug Love

Slip a tee onto the board. **1.** Cut a head from sparkly black felt and a body from red felt (pattern on page 30), and glue them on as shown. **2.** Use black satin cord for a center line and antennae. **3.** Glue on small black beads for the spots. Let dry.

Giant Dragonfly

Slip a tee onto the board. **1.** Cut a narrow oval from sparkly green felt, and glue it on the tee. **2.** Add large, small, and teardrop-shaped purple and green gems as shown. **3.** Cut pieces off a silver snowflake sequin and glue them on for antennae. Let dry.

Sun and Moon

Sky-high shirts for sleepovers, science fairs, and space camp

Sunshine Sky

Slip a tee onto the board. **1.** Cut a sun from yellow felt (pattern on page 30), and glue it to the tee. **2.** Add a large, round yellow gem to the center. Let dry.

Silvery Moon

Slip a tee onto the board. **1.** Cut out white felt clouds, and glue them to the tee as shown. **2.** Add star sequins and a silver moon sequin. Let dry.

Cheer Gear

Show-off sportswear for spirit rallies, sports, and surprise parties

Number One

Slip a tee onto the board. **1.** Cut strips of thin orange ribbon, and glue them to the tee as shown. **2.** For a "1," cut a wider orange ribbon strip as shown, and glue it on. Let dry.

Scream and Shout

Slip a tee onto the board. **1.** For a megaphone, cut a triangle from sparkly green felt, end pieces from sparkly blue felt, and a handle and sound waves from green satin cord. **2.** Glue all the pieces together as shown. Let dry.

Shooting Star

Slip a tee onto the board. Glue on a silver star rhinestone bead and small blue gems as shown. Let dry.

Name-Dropper

Flashy fashions for first days, friendships, and family reunions

Love Letters

Slip a tee onto the board. **1.** Trace a capital letter from a font or hand-draw the first initial of your doll's name onto sparkly blue felt. Cut out. **2.** Glue the letter to the tee. Let dry.

Mini Monogram

Slip a tee onto the board.
1. Glue a round iridescent sequin on the upper left side of the tee. **2.** Glue your doll's initials in letter beads to the sequin. Let dry.

Vani-tee

Slip a tee onto the board.
1. Measure the tee from side seam to side seam. Cut a purple ribbon strip to fit and glue across chest. **2.** Glue your doll's name in letter beads to the ribbon. Let dry.

Summer Scenes

Brilliant basics for beachcombing, barbecues, and Bermuda

Flashy Fish

Slip a tee onto the board. 1. Glue a mix of seed beads along the bottom edge of the tee. 2. Cut out tiny triangles from sparkly blue and green felt, and glue them on as shown. 3. Add a blue or a green teardrop gem over each triangle point. Let dry.

Sun-brella

Slip a tee onto the board. 1. Glue a purple satin cord strip to the tee as shown. 2. Cut out an umbrella from sparkly purple felt (pattern on page 30), and glue it over the cord as shown. 3. Cut out wavy sand from tan felt and wavy water from sparkly blue felt, and glue them along the tee bottom as shown. Let dry.

Flip-Flop Top

Slip a tee onto the board. 1. Cut out flip-flops from sparkly green felt (pattern on page 30), and glue them to the tee. 2. For straps, glue on purple satin cord and purple gems. Let dry.

Winter Wonderful

Seasonal sparkle for snowboarding, sledding, and skiing

Silvery Snowflakes

Slip a tee onto the board. Glue iridescent and silver snowflake sequins to the tee. Let dry.

Mini Mittens

Slip a tee onto the board. 1. Cut out mittens from sparkly blue felt (pattern on page 30), and glue them to the tee. 2. Connect the mittens with black satin cord. 3. Cut cuffs from white felt, and glue them over the cord as shown. Let dry.

Frosty's Face

Slip a tee onto the board. 1. Glue on a white felt circle, bead eyes, and a sparkly orange felt nose. 2. For a hat, cut 3 sides off a large, round silver sequin, and use a cut side for a brim. 3. Glue on the hat as shown. Let dry.

Say Good Night

Darling designs for doodling, diary writing, and dreaming

Bunny Slippers

Slip a tee onto the board. **1.** Cut out an oval body and a rounded head from white felt, and cut tiny oval ears from pink felt. **2.** Glue pieces together on the tee as shown. **3.** Add clear seed beads for eyes and pink seed beads for noses. Let dry.

Sleep Sheep

Slip a tee onto the board. **1.** Cut out sheep
legs from black felt, and glue them on
as shown. **2.** Glue on the bottom rows of
white mini pom-poms. **3.** Cut out a head
from black felt (pattern on page 30), and
glue it so that the head rests over the pom-
poms. **4.** Finish with the top rows of pom-
poms, and glue on white seed-bead eyes.
Let dry.

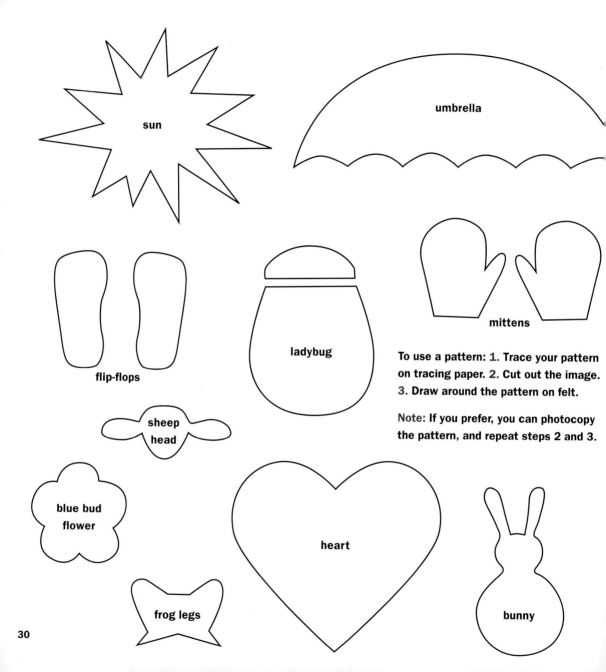

sun

umbrella

flip-flops

ladybug

mittens

To use a pattern: **1.** Trace your pattern on tracing paper. **2.** Cut out the image. **3.** Draw around the pattern on felt.

Note: If you prefer, you can photocopy the pattern, and repeat steps 2 and 3.

sheep head

blue bud flower

heart

frog legs

bunny

Show
us your
designs!

Show us your doll's favorite tee!
Send photo to:
Doll Tees Editor
American Girl
8400 Fairway Place
Middleton, WI 53562

(Photos can't be returned.
All comments and suggestions
received by American Girl Publishing
may be used without compensation
or acknowledgment.)

Here are some other American Girl books you might like:

❑ I read it.

❑ I read it.

❑ I read it.

❑ I read it.

❑ I read it.

❑ I read it.